How to Become a Loan Signing Agent

Lisa Carr

Published by Lisa Carr, 2024.

While every precaution has been taken in the preparation of this book, the publisher assumes no responsibility for errors or omissions, or for damages resulting from the use of the information contained herein.

HOW TO BECOME A LOAN SIGNING AGENT

First edition. March 10, 2024.

Copyright © 2024 Lisa Carr.

ISBN: 979-8224409273

Written by Lisa Carr.

Table of Contents

CHAPTER 1 – THE ROLE OF A SIGNING AGENT

The role of a loan signing agent is crucial in the real estate and mortgage industry. When individuals or businesses take out a loan for purchasing or refinancing a property, there's a significant amount of paperwork involved. A loan signing agent acts as a neutral third-party witness who facilitates the signing of these documents and ensures that the process is executed smoothly and accurately.

Overview of the Loan Signing Process

Here are the key responsibilities and functions of a loan signing agent:

Document Presentation:

The loan signing agent receives loan documents from the Lender, Title Company, or signing service. They carefully review these documents to ensure completeness and accuracy before presenting them to the customer for signing.

Signing Appointment:

The agent schedules a convenient time and place for the customer to sign the loan documents. This could be at the customer's home, workplace, or another agreed-upon location.

Identification Verification:

Before proceeding with the signing, the loan signing agent verifies the identity of the customer by checking their government-issued identification, such as a driver's license or passport.

Explaining Documents:

While the loan signing agent cannot provide legal advice, they are responsible for explaining the purpose and significance of each document to the customer. They ensure that the customer understands what they are signing and can answer any questions regarding the documents as it relates to where questions. You should be able to identify "where" in the documents the customer can find the answer to their question.

Witnessing Signatures:

The agent witnesses the customer's signature on each document requiring execution. They ensure that the signatures are placed in the correct locations and that the documents are signed as required by law per your State's regulations.

Notarization:

Some loan documents may require notarization. In such cases, the loan signing agent acts as a notary public and performs the notarization process, including verifying the identity of the signer and administering the oath, affirmation or acknowledgement.

Document Return:

After the signing appointment, the loan signing agent ensures that all signed documents are returned promptly to the appropriate parties, such as the Lender or Title Company according to the specific label provided.

Accuracy and Attention to Detail:

Throughout the signing process, the loan signing agent must maintain a high level of accuracy and attention to detail. Mistakes or errors in the signing process can have significant legal and financial consequences.

Neutrality and Impartiality:

As a neutral third-party witness, the loan signing agent must remain impartial and unbiased throughout the signing process. They cannot favor one party over another and must act in accordance with ethical standards and professional integrity and you most definitely cannot give advice.

Overall, the role of a loan signing agent is to facilitate the loan closing process by ensuring that all necessary documents are properly executed and legally binding. Their expertise and attention to detail help streamline the transaction and provide peace of mind to all parties involved.

CHAPTER 2 – WHY BECOME A SIGNING AGENT

Becoming a loan signing agent offers several compelling reasons for individuals looking to enter the real estate and mortgage industry or seeking a flexible and rewarding career path. Here are some key motivations:

Flexibility:

One of the primary reasons to become a loan signing agent is the flexibility it offers. As an independent contractor, you have control over your schedule and can choose when and where to work. This flexibility is especially appealing to individuals who need to balance work with other commitments, such as family responsibilities or pursuing further education.

Lucrative Income Potential:

Loan signing agents typically earn fees for each signing they conduct, and the income potential can be substantial. While earnings vary depending on factors such as location, experience, and the number of signings completed, many loan signing agents enjoy a lucrative income that can rival or even exceed that of traditional full-time employment.

Low Barrier to Entry:

Unlike many other professions in the real estate and mortgage industry that require extensive education or licensure, becoming a loan signing agent often has a relatively low barrier to entry. While obtaining training and certification is recommended, it does not require years of study or substantial financial investment.

High Demand:

The demand for loan signing agents remains consistently high, driven by the ongoing need for real estate transactions, refinancing, and mortgage-related activities. As long as people continue to buy and sell properties or refinance their mortgages, there will be a need for loan signing services.

Minimal Overhead Costs:

Another advantage of becoming a loan signing agent is the minimal overhead costs associated with the business. Unlike other entrepreneurial ventures that may require significant upfront investments in equipment, inventory, or office space, loan signing agents can operate with minimal overhead, often working from a home office with just a few essential tools.

Entrepreneurial Opportunity:

For individuals who enjoy entrepreneurship and the autonomy it brings, becoming a loan signing agent offers an excellent opportunity to run your own business. You have the freedom to market your services, build relationships with clients, and grow your business according to your goals and aspirations.

Rewarding Work:

Many loan signing agents find their work to be personally rewarding. They play a vital role in facilitating real estate transactions, helping clients achieve their homeownership goals, and contributing to the smooth and efficient functioning of the mortgage industry. This sense of fulfillment can be a significant motivator for those considering a career as a loan signing agent.

Overall, becoming a loan signing agent can be an attractive career choice for individuals seeking flexibility, financial opportunity, and the satisfaction of helping others navigate the complex process of buying or refinancing a home.

Assess your Skills and Qualifications:

Assessing your skills and qualifications is a crucial first step in becoming a successful loan signing agent. Here are some key areas to consider:

Attention to Detail:

Loan documents are complex and often contain legal terminology. A keen attention to detail is essential to ensure that all documents are accurately reviewed, explained, and signed during the loan signing process.

Communication Skills:

As a loan signing agent, you will interact with customers from diverse backgrounds. Strong communication skills are necessary to explain complex concepts clearly, answer questions effectively, and build rapport with clients.

Organizational Skills:

Managing multiple signings, scheduling appointments, and keeping track of documents require strong organizational skills. You should be able to stay organized and maintain attention to detail while juggling various tasks.

Customer Service:

Providing excellent customer service is essential for building relationships with clients and earning referrals. You should be friendly, professional, and responsive to clients' needs throughout the signing process.

Ethical Conduct:

Loan signing agents must adhere to ethical standards and maintain confidentiality throughout the signing process. Upholding integrity and professionalism is essential to earning trust and credibility in the industry.

Time Management:

Meeting deadlines and managing appointments efficiently is critical as a loan signing agent. You should be able to prioritize tasks, manage your time effectively, and ensure that signings are completed on schedule.

Computer Literacy:

While not always required, basic computer skills are beneficial for managing electronic documents, communicating with clients, and accessing online resources related to loan signing. Title companies and Lenders will each have their unique portal for the purposes of uploading loan documents in PDF format. It will be essential as a signing agent to have the basic understanding of Adobe and how to navigate the respective portals.

Legal Knowledge (Optional):

While loan signing agents cannot provide legal advice, having a basic understanding of real estate and mortgage terminology can be advantageous. Consider taking courses or obtaining certifications to enhance your knowledge in this area.

Flexibility:

Loan signings may occur during evenings, weekends, or holidays, depending on clients' schedules. Flexibility in your availability is essential to accommodate clients' needs and maximize opportunities for signings.

Continuous Learning:

The real estate and mortgage industry is constantly evolving, with new regulations and procedures introduced regularly. Commit to ongoing learning and professional development to stay current with industry trends and best practices.

CHAPTER 3 – UNDERSTANDING STATE REQUIREMENTS AND REGULATIONS

Understanding state requirements and regulations is essential for anyone considering a career as a loan signing agent. Each state has its own set of laws, regulations, and licensing requirements governing the practice of loan signing, so it's crucial to familiarize yourself with the specific rules in your state. Here's how to navigate this process:

Research State Regulations:

Start by researching the laws and regulations governing loan signing agents in your state. You can typically find this information on the website of your state's department of real estate or equivalent regulatory agency. Look for specific requirements related to licensing, training, bonding, insurance, and any other relevant regulations.

Licensing Requirements:

Some states require loan signing agents to obtain a license or certification before they can conduct signings. Determine whether your state has any licensing requirements for loan signing agents, and if so, familiarize yourself with the application process, fees, and any continuing education requirements.

Training Requirements:

Even in states where licensing is not required, completing training courses in loan signing is highly recommended. Look for reputable training programs that cover essential topics such as document preparation, identification verification, notarization procedures, and legal requirements. Many online and in-person courses are available to help you acquire the necessary skills and knowledge.

Bonding and Insurance:

Depending on your state's regulations, you may be required to obtain a surety bond or liability insurance as a loan signing agent. These financial protections help safeguard clients and ensure compliance with state laws. Be sure to understand the bonding and insurance requirements in your state and obtain the necessary coverage as required. Based on my experience, a minimum of $25,000 Errors and Omissions Insurance is required by Title companies.

Background Check:

Annual background checks have become standard practice in the loan signing industry, with many signing agencies and clients requiring them as part of their due diligence process. Background checks help mitigate potential risks associated with hiring signing agents, such as fraud, identity theft, or negligence. By screening for criminal history, financial stability, and other relevant factors, clients can reduce the likelihood of legal or financial liabilities stemming from the actions of the signing agent.

Notary Public Commission:

Loan signing agents are also commissioned as notary publics, allowing them to perform notarizations as part of the signing process. If your state requires notary commission, familiarize yourself with the requirements and application process for becoming a notary public, including any education or training requirements and fees.

Continuing Education:

Stay informed about any changes or updates to state regulations governing loan signing by participating in continuing education courses or staying connected with industry associations and professional organizations. Many states require loan signing agents to complete ongoing education to maintain their licenses or certifications. This is also a requirement of most Lenders and title companies.

Compliance with Federal Laws:

In addition to state regulations, loan signing agents must also comply with federal laws governing real estate transactions and mortgage lending, such as the Truth in Lending Act (TILA), Real Estate Settlement Procedures Act (RESPA), and Fair Housing Act. Familiarize yourself with these federal laws and their implications for loan signing activities.

By thoroughly understanding state requirements and regulations, you can ensure that you are properly licensed, trained, and compliant with all applicable laws as a loan signing agent. This not only helps protect you and your clients but also enhances your credibility and professionalism in the industry.

Education and Training

Enrolling in loan signing courses is a crucial step in preparing for a career as a loan signing agent. These courses provide essential training and knowledge necessary to perform the duties of a loan signing agent effectively and efficiently. Here's how to go about enrolling in loan signing courses:

Research Course Providers:

Start by researching reputable course providers that offer comprehensive training in loan signing. Look for providers with a track record of delivering high-quality, up-to-date content and positive reviews from past students. Consider factors such as course content, instructor credentials, and student support services.

Course Curriculum

Review the curriculum of each course to ensure it covers essential topics relevant to loan signing, such as document preparation, identification verification, notarization procedures, legal requirements, and industry best practices. Look for courses that provide practical, hands-on training and real-world examples to help you develop the necessary skills.

Delivery Format:

Consider the delivery format of the course, whether it's online, in-person, or a combination of both. Online courses offer flexibility and convenience, allowing you to study at your own pace from anywhere with an internet connection. In-person courses may provide opportunities for hands-on practice and interaction with instructors and fellow students.

Course Duration and Schedule:

Determine the duration and schedule of the course to ensure it fits your availability and learning preferences. Some courses may be completed in a few days or weeks, while others may span several months. Choose a course that aligns with your schedule and allows you to balance your other commitments effectively.

Cost and Fees:

Consider the cost of the course, including any registration fees, materials, and additional expenses. Compare the costs of different courses to ensure you're getting value for your investment. Keep in mind that higher-priced courses may offer more comprehensive content or additional features, so weigh the benefits against the cost.

Accreditation and Certification:

Look for courses that are accredited by reputable organizations or industry associations, as this can enhance the credibility and recognition of your training. Some courses may also offer certification upon completion, which can demonstrate your competence and professionalism to potential clients and employers.

Student Support and Resources:

Evaluate the level of student support and resources provided by the course provider, such as instructor assistance, online forums, study guides, and practice materials. Access to additional resources can help reinforce your learning and prepare you for success as a loan signing agent.

Read Reviews and Testimonials:

Before enrolling in a course, read reviews and testimonials from past students to get an idea of their experiences and satisfaction with the training. Positive reviews can indicate that the course is well-regarded and effective in preparing students for a career in loan signing.

Once you've selected a loan signing course that meets your needs and preferences, complete the enrollment process according to the instructions provided by the course provider. Take advantage of the opportunity to learn and acquire the knowledge and skills necessary to excel as a loan signing agent.

CHAPTER 4 – ONLINE RESOURCES AND TRAINING PROGRAMS

There are several online resources and training programs available to individuals interested in becoming loan signing agents. These resources offer comprehensive training, certification, and support to help you develop the necessary skills and knowledge for success in this field. Here are some popular online resources and training programs:

National Notary Association (NNA):

The NNA offers a variety of online training courses and resources for loan signing agents. Their Loan Signing Agent Certification Course covers essential topics such as document preparation, identification verification, notarization procedures, and industry best practices. The NNA also provides additional resources, such as webinars, articles, and practice exams, to support your learning. They are the most recognized by Lenders and title companies.

Loan Signing System:

The Loan Signing System, created by Mark Wills, is a popular online training program for aspiring loan signing agents. This comprehensive course covers everything you need to know to start and grow your loan signing business, including step-by-step instruction, real-world examples, and ongoing support. The course includes video tutorials, downloadable materials, and live coaching sessions to help you master the skills required for success.

123notary.com:

123notary.com offers a range of online training materials and resources for loan signing agents. Their Signing Agent Training Course covers essential topics such as loan documents, signing procedures, notarization requirements, and marketing strategies. The course is self-paced and includes interactive modules, quizzes, and downloadable resources to support your learning.

Notary2Pro:

Notary2Pro provides online training and certification programs for notaries and loan signing agents. Their Signing Agent Certification Course covers the fundamentals of loan signing, including document preparation, identification verification, notarization procedures, and industry standards. The course is self-paced and includes video instruction, quizzes, and hands-on exercises to help you build your skills.

YouTube Channels:

Several YouTube channels offer free tutorials, tips, and resources for loan signing agents. Channels such as Loan Signing System, Notary Coach, and Sign & Thrive provide valuable insights, training videos, and interviews with industry experts to help you improve your skills and stay updated on industry trends.

CHAPTER 5 – HANDS-ON TRAINING OPPORTUNITIES

Hands-on training opportunities are invaluable for individuals aspiring to become loan signing agents. While online courses provide theoretical knowledge, hands-on training allows you to apply that knowledge in real-world scenarios, gaining practical experience and confidence in your abilities. Here are some ways to find hands-on training opportunities:

Local Notary Associations:

Check if there are any notary associations or organizations in your area that offer hands-on training sessions or workshops for loan signing agents. These associations may host events where you can practice signing techniques, learn from experienced professionals, and network with industry peers.

Notary Public Seminars:

Look for notary public seminars or conferences in your area that include sessions specifically focused on loan signing. These events often feature hands-on workshops, role-playing exercises, and interactive demonstrations to help you develop your skills as a loan signing agent.

Mentorship Programs:

Consider seeking out mentorship opportunities with experienced loan signing agents who are willing to provide guidance and hands-on training. Mentors can offer valuable insights, share practical tips, and accompany you to signings to observe and learn from their expertise.

Title Companies and Escrow Agencies:

Reach out to local title companies and escrow agencies to inquire about shadowing opportunities or internships for aspiring loan signing agents. Some companies may allow you to accompany seasoned signing agents on signings, providing valuable hands-on experience and exposure to the signing process.

Networking Events:

Attend networking events, industry conferences, and meetups where loan signing agents and industry professionals gather. These events offer opportunities to connect with experienced agents, learn from their experiences, and potentially arrange hands-on training or mentoring relationships.

Continuing Education Courses:

Many notary associations and training providers offer advanced or specialized courses for loan signing agents that include hands-on components. Look for courses that incorporate practical exercises, case studies, and role-playing scenarios to enhance your skills and confidence in conducting signings.

Online Platforms:

Some online platforms offer virtual or simulated signing experiences that replicate real-world signing scenarios. While not a substitute for hands-on training, these platforms can supplement your learning and provide opportunities to practice your skills in a controlled environment.

When seeking hands-on training opportunities, be proactive in reaching out to industry professionals, attending relevant events, and actively engaging in your learning journey. Hands-on experience is essential for mastering the intricacies of loan signing and preparing you for success in your career as a loan signing agent.

CHAPTER 6 – CHOOSING A BUSINESS STRUCTURE

Choosing the right business structure is an important decision for anyone starting a loan signing agent business. The structure you choose will impact various aspects of your business, including taxation, liability, and operational flexibility. Here are some common business structures to consider:

Sole Proprietorship:

A sole proprietorship is the simplest and most common form of business structure. In this setup, you are the sole owner and operator of the business, and there is no legal distinction between you and the business entity. While easy to set up and operate, a sole proprietorship offers no protection from personal liability for business debts or legal obligations.

Limited Liability Company (LLC):

An LLC is a popular choice for small businesses, offering a balance of simplicity and liability protection. As an LLC owner, you enjoy limited liability, meaning your personal assets are protected from business debts and liabilities. LLCs also offer flexibility in terms of taxation, allowing you to choose how you want the business to be taxed (as a sole proprietorship, partnership, or corporation).

Partnership:

If you are starting the loan signing agent business with one or more partners, a partnership structure may be appropriate. There are two main types of partnerships: general partnerships, where all partners share equally in the profits and liabilities of the business, and limited partnerships, where one or more partners have limited liability but may not participate in the day-to-day operations of the business.

Corporation:

A corporation is a separate legal entity from its owners, offering the highest level of personal liability protection. However, corporations are more complex and expensive to set up and maintain compared to other business structures. They are subject to double taxation, meaning that profits are taxed at both the corporate level and the individual level when distributed to shareholders as dividends.

Professional Corporation (PC) or Professional Limited Liability Company (PLLC):

If you are required to hold a professional license or certification to operate as a loan signing agent in your state, you may be required to form a professional corporation (PC) or professional limited liability company (PLLC). These structures are similar to regular corporations or LLCs but are specifically designed for licensed professionals.

When choosing a business structure for your loan signing agent business, consider factors such as the level of personal liability protection you need, the complexity of the business, taxation implications, and regulatory requirements in your state. It's advisable to consult with a legal or financial advisor to evaluate your options and determine the best structure for your specific circumstances.

CHAPTER 7 – SETTING UP YOUR OFFICE

Setting up your office as a loan signing agent is essential for creating a professional and efficient workspace where you can conduct signings, manage paperwork, and communicate with clients. Here are some steps to consider when setting up your office:

Choose a Dedicated Space:

Designate a specific area of your home or commercial space as your office. Ideally, this space should be quiet, well-lit, and free from distractions to help you focus on your work. If possible, select a room with a door that can be closed to provide privacy for clients' information.

Invest in Essential Equipment:

Equip your office with the necessary tools and equipment to conduct signings effectively. This may include a reliable computer or laptop, printer, scanner, copier, fax machine, and mobile device for communication. Consider investing in a high-quality printer capable of printing legal-sized documents and a scanner with document feeder for efficient scanning of multiple pages.

A laser printer is the required printer for most Lenders and title companies. Get yourself a dual tray printer that can accommodate both letter and legal size paper. You will be required to scan documents more than half the time so it is highly recommended you invest in an efficient scanner and mobile scanner.

Arrange Furniture and Layout:

Arrange your office furniture in a way that promotes productivity and professionalism. Invest in a comfortable desk and ergonomic chair where you can work comfortably for extended periods. Organize your workspace with filing cabinets, shelves, or storage bins to keep documents, supplies, and equipment neatly organized and easily accessible.

Set up Technology and Communication Tools:

Ensure you have access to reliable internet connectivity and phone service in your office. Set up a dedicated business phone line or use a separate mobile phone for professional calls. Consider installing a dedicated business email address and setting up a professional voicemail greeting to enhance your professional image.

Ensure Compliance with Regulations:

Familiarize yourself with any regulatory requirements or guidelines governing the setup of your office as a loan signing agent. Ensure that your office meets all legal and professional standards, including privacy and confidentiality requirements for handling sensitive client information.

By following these steps, you can create a functional and professional office space that supports your success as a loan signing agent and provides a comfortable and efficient environment for conducting signings and managing your business operations.

CHAPTER 8 – ACQUIRING NECESSARY EQUIPMENT AND SUPPLIES

Acquiring the necessary equipment and supplies is essential for setting up your office as a loan signing agent and conducting signings efficiently. Here's a list of essential equipment and supplies you'll need:

Computer or Laptop:

A reliable computer or laptop is essential for accessing loan documents, communicating with clients, and managing your business operations. Choose a device with sufficient processing power, memory, and storage capacity to handle your workload effectively.

Printer:

Invest in a high-quality printer capable of printing legal-sized documents. Choose a printer with fast printing speeds, and reliable performance to ensure professional-quality prints for your signings. A laser printer is the required printer by Lenders and title companies. As previously mentioned, invest in a dual tray printer as most packages comprise of mixed page sizes.

Scanner:

A scanner with a document feeder is essential for scanning signed documents and returning them to clients electronically. Look for a scanner with fast scanning speeds, automatic document detection, and high-resolution scanning capabilities for clear and accurate scans.

Mobile Device:

A mobile device, such as a smart phone or tablet, is useful for staying connected while on the go. Use your mobile device to communicate with clients, access digital documents, and manage appointments and schedules.

Notary Seal and Stamp:

As a commissioned notary public, you will need to obtain a notary seal and stamp (check your State's requirements) for notarizing documents during signings. Ensure that your seal and stamp comply with state regulations and include all required information, such as your name, commission expiration date, and notary identification number.

Office Supplies:

Stock up on essential office supplies, including pens, sign-here stickers, paper clips, file folders and rubber bands. Having these supplies on hand ensures that you're prepared for signings and can provide clients with the tools they need to complete paperwork. Have on hand a supply of polypak envelopes for both UPS and FedEx. They are free to order from each of their websites.

Business Cards:

Create professional business cards with your contact information, business name, and logo to provide to clients and network with industry contacts. Business cards are a valuable marketing tool for promoting your services and establishing your brand identity as a loan signing agent.

Internet Connectivity:

Ensure you have access to reliable internet connectivity in your office to access online resources, communicate with clients, and download digital documents. Consider investing in a high-speed internet connection with sufficient bandwidth to support your business needs.

Backup Power Supply:

To prevent disruptions during signings, consider investing in a backup power supply, such as an uninterruptible power supply (UPS) or portable generator. Backup power ensures that your equipment remains operational during power outages or emergencies, allowing you to complete signings without interruption.

By acquiring the necessary equipment and supplies, you can set up your office as a loan signing agent and conduct signings efficiently and professionally. Be sure to invest in high-quality equipment and stock up on essential supplies to support your business operations and provide clients with the best possible experience.

CHAPTER 9 – PRACTICING PROPER IDENTIFICATION VERFICATION TECHNIQUES

Practicing proper identification verification techniques is essential for loan signing agents to ensure the integrity and legality of the signing process. Here are some best practices for verifying identification effectively:

Review Identification Documents:

Ask the signer to provide valid government-issued identification, such as a driver's license, passport, or state-issued ID card. Review the identification document carefully to ensure it is current, unexpired, and contains a recognizable photo of the signer.

Verify Name and Signature:

Compare the name and signature on the identification document with the name and signature on the loan documents. Ensure that the names match exactly and that the signature on the identification document resembles the signature on the loan documents. Some Lenders will require signer to sign exactly name appears on documents. Review your instructions prior to appointment.

Check Expiration Date:

Verify that the identification document has not expired. Some forms of identification, such as driver's licenses and passports, have expiration dates that must be current for the document to be considered valid.

Look for Security Features:

Examine the identification document for security features such as holograms, watermarks, or special markings that indicate authenticity. Familiarize yourself with the security features of commonly used identification documents to detect potential signs of forgery or tampering.

Verify Physical Description:

Compare the physical description of the signer on the identification document (e.g., height, weight, hair color) with the signer's appearance in person. Ensure that the physical characteristics match or are consistent with the information provided on the identification document.

Confirm Issuing Authority:

Verify the issuing authority of the identification document to ensure it is valid and recognized by government agencies. Different states and countries may issue different types of identification, so be familiar with the various forms of acceptable identification in your area.

Check for Alterations or Damage:

Inspect the identification document for any signs of alterations, damage, or tampering. Look for discrepancies in the information presented, such as changes to the name or expiration date, which may indicate fraudulent activity.

Document Verification Process:

Keep detailed records of the identification verification process, including the type of identification provided, the date and time of verification, and any relevant notes or observations. Documenting your verification process helps demonstrate compliance with legal and regulatory requirements.

Most States mandate a journal for all notarizations. Even if your State does not require a journal, it is highly recommended to maintain one so as to keep proper records for all of your notarizations.

Continuously Educate Yourself:

Stay informed about updates to identification documents and security features by participating in training courses, attending workshops, and staying connected with industry associations. Continuous education and professional development are essential for maintaining proficiency in identification verification techniques.

By following these best practices and exercising diligence and attention to detail, loan signing agents can effectively verify identification and ensure the legitimacy of the signing process. Proper identification verification helps protect against identity theft, fraud, and legal disputes, promoting trust and confidence in the loan signing process.

CHAPTER 10- MAINTAINING RECORDS AND DOCUMENTATIONS

Maintain Confidentiality and Security:

Take measures to safeguard sensitive client information and maintain confidentiality and privacy. Store physical documents in locked filing cabinets or secure storage areas and use password protection and encryption for digital files stored on computers or cloud-based platforms.

Back Up Date Regularly:

Implement a regular backup schedule to protect against data loss or system failures. Backup digital files and records regularly to external hard drives, cloud storage services, or secure servers to ensure redundancy and availability of critical information.

Track Business Expenses:

Keep detailed records of business expenses, including receipts, invoices, and payment records, to track income and expenses accurately. Categorize expenses by type (e.g., office supplies, mileage, marketing) and maintain records of deductible expenses for tax purposes.

Document Notarial Acts:

Maintain accurate records of notarial acts performed, including notary journals, logbooks, or electronic notary records. Record relevant information such as the date, time, location, type of notarization, identification of signers, and any fees charged for services rendered.

CHAPTER 11 – DEALING WITH DIFFICULT SIGNINGS

Dealing with difficult signings can be challenging, but it's essential to remain calm, professional, and focused on resolving the situation effectively. Here are some strategies for handling difficult signings:

Stay Calm and Composed:

Maintain your composure and remain calm, even in challenging or stressful situations. Take deep breaths, stay focused on the task at hand, and avoid reacting emotionally to difficult clients or unexpected issues.

Listen Actively:

Practice active listening by giving your full attention to the client and acknowledging their concerns or frustrations. Let the client express their thoughts and feelings without interruption, and demonstrate empathy and understanding for their perspective.

Clarify Expectations:

Clarify expectations with the client regarding the signing process, timelines, and any specific requirements or preferences they may have. Ensure that both parties have a clear understanding of what to expect and how the signing will proceed to minimize misunderstandings or miscommunication.

Seek Assistance if Needed:

Do not hesitate to contact your hiring party or Lender if you encounter difficulties during a signing. Halt the signing and seek a resolution as much as possible.

CHAPTER 12- HANDLING ERRORS AND CORRECTIONS

Handling errors and corrections during loan signings is an important aspect of maintaining professionalism and ensuring accuracy in the signing process. Here are some strategies for effectively managing errors and making corrections:

Acknowledge the Error:

Acknowledge the error or mistake openly and honestly with the client. Take responsibility for the error, and reassure the client that you are committed to resolving the issue promptly and effectively.

Apologize Sincerely:

Offer a sincere apology to the client for any inconvenience or confusion caused by the error. Express empathy and understanding for the client's concerns, and assure them that you are committed to addressing the issue and providing a satisfactory resolution.

Take Immediate Action:

Take immediate action to correct the error and minimize any potential impact on the signing process. Determine the appropriate course of action based on the nature and severity of the error, and implement corrective measures promptly to rectify the mistake.

Re-Review Documents:

Re-review the signing documents carefully after making corrections to ensure that all errors have been addressed and that the documents are accurate and complete. Verify the accuracy of the corrected information and confirm that all necessary signatures and initials are present.

CHAPTER 13 – EXPANDING YOUR SERVICE OFFERINGS

Expanding your service offerings as a loan signing agent can help diversify your income streams, attract new clients, and differentiate yourself in the market. Here are some strategies for expanding your service offerings:

Additional Notarial Services:

Consider offering additional notarial services beyond loan signings, such as acknowledgments, jurats, affidavits, or power of attorney signings. Expand your expertise and certification to provide a broader range of notarial services to clients in various industries.

Mobile Notary Services:

Offer mobile notary services to clients who require document notarization at their location, such as homes, offices, hospitals, or assisted living facilities. Provide convenience and flexibility by traveling to clients' preferred locations for notarial appointments.

Remote Online Notarization (RON):

Obtain certification to perform remote online notarization (RON) services, allowing you to notarize documents electronically via secure online platforms. Expand your reach and accessibility by offering RON services to clients located anywhere within your authorized jurisdiction.

Document Preparation Assistance:

Provide document preparation assistance to clients who need help completing or reviewing legal documents, loan applications, or other paperwork related to real estate transactions. Offer guidance and support to clients throughout the document preparation process to ensure accuracy and completeness.

Multilingual Services:

If you're fluent in multiple languages, offer multilingual signing services to clients who prefer or require documents to be notarized in languages other than English. Cater to diverse client demographics and expand your market reach by offering services in additional languages.

Specialized Niche Services:

Identify specialized niches or markets within the loan signing industry, such as commercial real estate, reverse mortgages, weddings or estate planning, and tailor your services to meet the unique needs of clients in these sectors. Develop expertise in specialized areas to differentiate yourself and attract niche clientele.

By expanding your service offerings strategically, loan signing agents can diversify their revenue streams, broaden their client base, and position themselves for long-term success and growth in the competitive loan signing industry. Evaluate your skills, interests, and market opportunities to identify areas for expansion and innovation that align with your business goals and objectives.

CHAPTER 14 – USEFUL WEBSITES AND ONLINE COMMUNITIES

National Notary Association (NNA):

The NNA is a leading organization for notaries and signing agents, offering a wealth of resources, training programs, and industry updates. Their website provides access to educational materials, certification courses, and networking opportunities for professionals in the field.

123notary.com:

123notary.com is a popular online directory and resource hub for notaries and signing agents. It offers a comprehensive database of signing agents, educational resources, and forums for discussing industry-related topics and networking with other professionals.

Notary Rotary:

Notary Rotary is a community-driven website that provides a range of resources and tools for notaries and signing agents. It offers forums, discussion boards, and a marketplace for connecting with other professionals and accessing educational materials and supplies.

Loan Signing System Community:

The Loan Signing System Community, founded by Mark Wills, provides a platform for loan signing agents to connect, share insights, and access training resources. It offers forums, webinars, and networking opportunities for members looking to grow their businesses and expand their skills.

SigningAgent.com:

SigningAgent.com is a website dedicated to connecting signing agents with signing services, title companies, and Lenders. It offers a directory of signing agents, educational resources, and networking opportunities for professionals in the industry.

LinkedIn:

LinkedIn is a valuable platform for networking and professional development in the loan signing industry. Join relevant groups, connect with other signing agents and industry professionals, and participate in discussions to expand your network and stay updated on industry trends and opportunities.

Facebook Groups:

There are several Facebook groups dedicated to notaries and loan signing agents, where members can share tips, ask questions, and connect with peers. Search for groups such as "Loan Signing Agents," "Notary Public Network," or "Notary Signing Agent Forum" to join relevant communities.

Reddit:

Reddit hosts several subreddits related to notaries and loan signing agents, where members can discuss industry topics, share resources, and ask for advice. Check out subreddits such as r/Notary, r/LoanSigning, or r/NotarySigningAgents to join the conversation.

Local Notary Associations:

Many states and regions have local notary associations or organizations that offer networking events, educational seminars, and resources for notaries and signing agents. Check with your local notary association or chamber of commerce to find opportunities for connecting with other professionals in your area.

Professional Forums and Blogs:

Explore professional forums, blogs, and websites dedicated to notaries and loan signing agents for valuable insights, tips, and resources. Websites such as Notary Café, NotaryCoach.com, and Notary.net offer educational content, forums, and community resources for professionals in the industry. These websites and online communities provide valuable resources, networking opportunities, and support for loan signing agents looking to expand their knowledge, grow their businesses, and connect with other professionals in the industry.

CHAPTER 15 – ESSENTIAL TOOLS AND SOFTWARE FOR LOAN SIGNING AGENTS

Notary Software:

Invest in notary software specifically designed for notaries and signing agents to streamline document management, track signings, and maintain compliance with legal requirements. Notary software solutions like Notarize or NotaryGadget which offer features such as document storage, and notary journals.

Mobile Scanning Apps:

Install mobile scanning apps on your smartphone or tablet to capture high-quality scans of documents on the go. Apps like Adobe Scan, CamScanner, or Scanbot enable you to digitize documents, convert them into PDFs, and share them electronically with clients or Lenders.

Remote Online Notarization (RON) Platforms:

If certified to perform remote online notarization (RON), use RON platforms like Notarize, Pavaso, or Nexsys Clear Sign to conduct electronic notarizations remotely. These platforms enable you to notarize documents online, verify signer identities, and maintain a secure digital record of the notarization process.

Mobile Notary Bag or Kit:

Equip yourself with a mobile notary bag or kit containing essential tools, supplies, and resources for conducting signings on the go. Include items such as pens, notary stamps, identification verification tools, business cards, and a portable scanner or printer to ensure you have everything you need for successful signings.

CHAPTER 16 – HOW TO BECOME A LOAN SIGNING AGENT

How to Become a Loan Signing Agent (LSA) or Notary Signing Agent (NSA)

BECOME A NOTARY PUBLIC

This is the foundation for your NSA career. Each state has specific requirements, but generally, you'll need to:

- Complete a notary education course covering notary laws and procedures.
- Get background checked
- Pass a notary public exam demonstrating your knowledge.
- Apply for a notary commission with your state government.
- Purchase a notary bond and errors and omissions (E&O) insurance. This protects you from financial liability if mistakes occur during notarization. A minimum insurance value of $25,000 is required by most Lenders and Title Companies. Premiums may vary.

Become NSA Certified

While not mandatory, NSA training polishes your skills and makes you a more attractive candidate to Lenders and Title Companies. Look for courses that cover:

- Loan signing procedures and best practices
- Common loan documents

- Customer service and communication skills for effectively guiding customers through the signing process
- Legal and ethical considerations specific to loan signings

National Notary Association and Loan Signing System are the two most recognized in the industry.

CHAPTER 17 – UNDERSTAND THE LOAN PROCESS FLOW

As a Loan Signing Agent, you do not "need" to know the following information. However, having this knowledge, not only builds your trust with title companies but it boosts your confidence when handling your closings. Clients rely on loan signing agents to provide professional expertise and guidance throughout the signing process. By understanding the loan flow process, agents can offer valuable insights, answer questions, and address client concerns confidently, enhancing the overall customer experience.

Types of Loans:

- Purchase – when one buys a home and obtains a mortgage
- Refinance – when one already has a mortgage and redoes the loan for various reasons, such as lowering interest rate or to take cash out
- Reverse mortgage – a product offered to a senior age group
- HELOC – home equity line of credit. It is a second mortgage on one's home
- Business Loans – loan given to a business for business purposes
- Auto Loans – for the purpose of purchasing a vehicle

The Process (summarized):

- Loan Application is submitted to mortgage broker or directly to a Lender
- Loan goes through an underwriting process
- Loan gets approved

- Loan gets sent off to various 3rd parties to process: appraisals, surveyors, credit etc
- Loan gets handed off to the Title Company. The Title Company also known as Settlement Agent or Closing Agent. They handle the final paperwork, such as, title searches and transfer of ownership.
- Customer signs final paperwork
- Loan gets funded and disbursed by the Title Company (not the Lender)
- Loan gets booked on Lender's portal
- Customer pays back loan

Overall, the process of applying for a mortgage involves multiple steps and requires careful planning, documentation, and coordination between the customer, Lender, Title Company and other parties involved. By understanding the flow of applying for a mortgage, NSAs can navigate the process more effectively and complete their signings with confidence.

CHAPTER 18 – YOUR FIRST CLOSING

L et's break it down.......

YOU RECEIVE A CALL, text message, or alert from a Title Company or signing agency

Signing orders can be received in several different formats. Some companies like Snapdocs will send out orders via text messages to several notaries in the area of the closing. You do not have much time to review order as it is a first come first serve basis for the most part.

Review the order carefully and quickly. It should state the date, time, location, type of order and fee. Over time, you will become versed in recognizing the key ingredients of the order to make your decision.

Ensure that you agree to all conditions and then accept the order. If you accepted an order that you are not able to fulfill, contact the hiring company immediately. Do not be afraid to do so. It happens to the best of us. However, do not let this become a habit.

Once you receive the order, you will then contact the customer to confirm the appointment. Once you have the customer on the phone, identify who you are, stating that you are the notary assigned to conduct the closing. Verify the date, time, location, all persons signing and ID requirements. Be specific. Ask for any parking or address clarifications. If leaving a text message, do not give out any personal information until you have permission from the customer to do so.

Inform customer that once loan package is received, if anything else is required, they will be contacted. The reason for this is that when you receive the loan package, you want to verify a few things:

- Verify all parties to sign will be present at closing if not already done so
- Verify if funds are due at closing
- Verify if witnesses are required

Be sure to read all notary instructions when package is received. Each Lender and Title Company is unique in their requirements. For instance, some require blue pens while some require black.

Print loan package according to PDF size. A dual tray printer is the most efficient and practical way to manage your printing needs. This will save you time and will also enhance your relationship with Title Companies.

Place sign here stickers throughout your package to ensure you do not miss any signatures or initials. You will not always need to this as you will become familiar with the documents as time goes on.

Place customer's copy in a file folder. Professionalism will go a long way.

WE WILL LOOK AT SOME of the most commonly used forms in a loan package.

A loan package can range anywhere from 75 to 250 pages. Take the time to go through the package prior to your closing so that you can familiarize yourself with each document, paying attention to any "new or unfamiliar" document. In order to have the smoothness transition during your closing, move the ID forms to the front of the package followed by the Closing Disclosure and ALTA Statement. I will explain later on.

The forms at the end are being explained from a loan signing agent point of view. Remember it is not your job to explain the "whys" or "hows" but you can point out the information on the document to the customer.

For instance, if a customer asks "what is their monthly payment?", you should know where to find that information.

I have included just a few at the end of this book for your review.

CHAPTER 19 – DAY OF CLOSING

Preparation is the key to a successful closing.

- Check that your loan package was printed accurately and no pages were cut off. Remember to print per PDF size
- Place the customer's copy in a file folder
- Check that your stamps are sufficiently inked
- Carry your journal
- Have extra pens – blue and black. Check for color requirement in your instructions.
- Have your mobile scanner and IPAD as necessary
- Read your instructions for scan back and return instructions
- Head to your closing. Make an effort to arrive at least 10 minutes early

During the Closing

Present yourself confidently. Clearly explain your role as the Signing Agent and assert your authority in guiding the signing process; restate that you are there to witness the closing. If during the closing there are questions related to the loan terms or any other legal questions, that you will refer them to the Title Company or Lender.

Control the closing.

Establish authority respectfully. Project confidence and professionalism throughout the closing process to instill trust and credibility with the customers. Manage the flow of the signing process. Keep distractions to a minimum, maintain a calm and focused demeanor, and ensure that all participants adhere to the timeline.

Verify IDs.

This is your first order of business. The Patriot Form will indicate if one or two forms of IDs are required. From time to time you will be given specific instructions from your hiring company. Those instructions are your go to. Follow proper identification verification procedures to ensure compliance with notarial requirements.

Start the closing.

You always start with the Closing Disclosure. Most times when you print the package, the Closing Disclosure is in the middle of the package. You do not want to start the closing, and then get to the Closing Disclosure, and now the customer has an issue with it. You would have wasted your time and theirs. Once the customer is happy with the numbers and everything is as agreed, the remainder of the package should go smoothly.

Notarize Documents and Complete Journal.

Notarize the necessary documents as required as you go. Ensure the notarial certificates are completed accurately and affixed with your official seal or stamp. There are times when the State and County are incorrect. You are to cross and initial and write the State and County where the notarization is taking place. Complete journal for every document notarized.

Errors on documents.

There are different types of errors that occur on the documents. Some errors may be corrected at the closing table, some may not. This is when you will place a call to the hiring company to determine how to proceed. Errors such as customer writing the date incorrectly or signing in the wrong location, should corrected by switching out the page with their copy. For any other errors, do not proceed with closing until you have clarified with Title Company or hiring agency on how to correct such errors.

Ensure Accuracy.

Double-check that all required fields are completed accurately, signatures are placed in the appropriate locations and dates are correct on each document. Verify that the customer's initials and signatures are consistent throughout the signing. After all documents have been signed, go back through the entire package to ensure that nothing was missed. This habit will save your time in the long run. Mistakes happen but they can be corrected if caught at the table.

Scan Package and Ship.

If scan back is required, do so immediately after closing. Having a mobile scanner allows you to do so from the closing table or if you're closing at an office, they may have the capability to accommodate scanning.

Once scans have been approved, place your package in a polypak (plastic) envelope and drop off at a brick and mortar location. Packages have been known to get lost in transit, so keep your receipt as your proof of delivery.

CONGRATULATIONS!!!!

You have completed your very first signing. This was no small feat, and it marks the beginning of an exciting and rewarding career in the loan signing industry.

CHAPTER 20 – HOW TO GET SIGNINGS

Getting signings as a loan signing agent requires a proactive approach to marketing and networking. Here are some effective strategies to help you get signings.

Build Relationships with Signing Services

Signing services act as intermediaries between signing agents and companies or individuals in need of loan signings. Reach out to signing services in your area and introduce yourself, highlighting your experience, professionalism, and availability for signings. Maintain regular contact and provide updates on your availability and credentials to stay top of mind.

Network with Title Companies and Lenders

Establish connections with local title companies, mortgage lenders, and real estate agents who may require signing services for their clients. Attend industry events, networking functions, and professional meetings to introduce yourself and build relationships with key decision-makers. Offer to provide your services on an as-needed basis and demonstrate your reliability and expertise.

Create an Online Presence

Create a professional website or online profile to showcase your services, experience, and credentials as a loan signing agent. Include client testimonials, and information about your availability and service area. Utilize social media platforms, such as LinkedIn, Facebook, and

Instagram, to promote your services, share industry insights, and connect with potential clients.

Join Signing Agent Directories

Register with signing agent directories and online marketplaces where companies and individuals can search for signing agents in their area. Ensure that your profile is complete, accurate, and up-to-date, including your contact information, service area, and availability for signings.

TOP 5 SIGNING AGENCIES

- SnapDocs
- Signing Order
- Notary Café
- SigningAgent.com
- Signature Closers

CHAPTER 21 – DOCUMENT SAMPLES

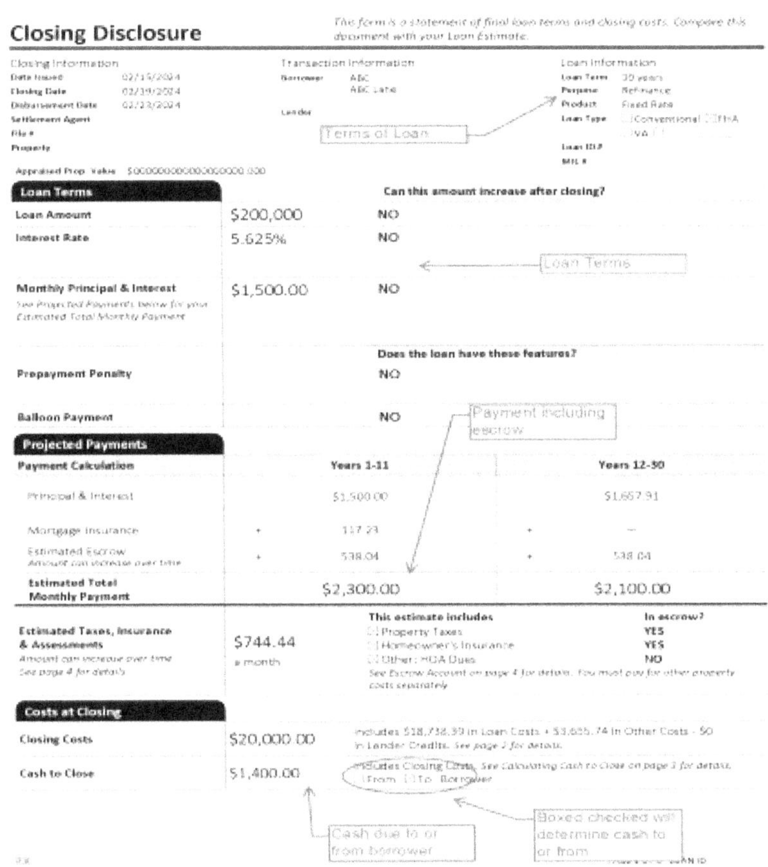

The Closing Disclosure (CD) is a key document provided to customers during the mortgage closing process. It outlines the final terms and costs associated with the mortgage loan, including details about the loan amount, interest rate, closing costs, and other fees. Typically 5-6 pages.

SAMPLE VERBIAGE:

"This is your Closing Disclosure". This document shows the terms of loan. This is a 30 year loan, FHA, this is your loan amount, rate, payment and final payment to include escrow. Below you will find the amount due to/from you. Once you have reviewed, please sign the last page, right above your name, where I have placed the sticker".

To be completed by the Lender:
Lender Loan No./Universal Loan Identifier]   Agency Case No. [

Uniform Residential Loan Application

Verify and complete the information on this application. If you are applying for this loan with others, each additional Borrower must provide information as directed by your Lender.

Section 1: Borrower Information. This section asks about your personal information and your income from employment and other sources, such as retirement, that you want considered to qualify for this loan.

1a. Personal Information

Name (First, Middle, Last, Suffix)

Alternate Names - List any names by which you are known or any names under which credit was previously received (First, Middle, Last, Suffix)

Social Security Number [
(or Individual Taxpayer Identification Number)

Date of Birth
(mm/dd/yyyy)
[

Citizenship
☉ U.S. Citizen
○ Permanent Resident Alien
○ Non-Permanent Resident Alien

Type of Credit
☉ I am applying for individual credit.
○ I am applying for joint credit. Total Number of Borrowers: ____
   Each Borrower intends to apply for joint credit.   Your initials: ______

List Name(s) of Other Borrower(s) Applying for this Loan
(First, Middle, Last, Suffix - Use a separator between names)

If joint application, initials are required Loan for the other section for the 2nd borrower.

Marital Status
☉ Married
○ Separated
○ Unmarried
   (Single, Divorced, Widowed, Civil Union, Domestic Partnership, Registered Reciprocal Beneficiary Relationship)

Dependents (not listed by another Borrower)
Number   0
Ages

Contact Information
Home Phone   (
Cell Phone   (
Work Phone   (
Email   yahoo.com

Current Address
Street ______________________________   Unit # _______
City ____________   State FL   ZIP ______   Country United States
How Long at Current Address? 10 Years ____ Months   Housing ○ No primary housing expense ☉ Own ○ Rent ($ ______ /month)

If at Current Address for LESS than 2 years, list Former Address   ☒ Does not apply

Mailing Address - if different from Current Address   ☒ Does not apply

1b. Current Employment/Self-Employment and Income   ☒ Does not apply

1c. IF APPLICABLE, Complete Information for Additional Employment/Self-Employment and Income   ☒ Does not apply

1d. IF APPLICABLE, Complete Information for Previous Employment/Self-Employment and Income   ☒ Does not apply
Provide at least 2 years of current and previous employment and income.

Borrower Name:
Uniform Residential Loan Application
Freddie Mac Form 65 • Fannie Mae Form 1003
Effective 1/2021

Page 1 of 59

THE LOAN APPLICATION is the customer's personal information and finances in which is used to qualify for the loan. Despite already having been approved, they must sign an original at closing.

SAMPLE VERBIAGE

"This is your loan application. A signed copy is required at closing. Please initial as indicated (only for joint applications) and sign and date on page......".

NOTE

[Date]   [City]   [State]

[Property Address]

1. **BORROWER'S PROMISE TO PAY**
   In return for a loan that I have received, I promise to pay U.S. $_______ (this amount is called "Principal")
   plus interest, to the order of the Lender. The Lender is [name of lender]

   [callout: loan amount]

   I will make all payments under this Note in the form of cash, check or money order.
   I understand that the Lender may transfer this Note. The Lender or anyone who takes this Note by transfer and who is entitled to receive payments under this Note is called the "Note Holder."

2. **INTEREST**   *[callout: interest rate]*
   Interest will be charged on unpaid principal until the full amount of Principal has been paid. I will pay interest at a yearly rate of **3.875 %**.
   The interest rate required by this Section 2 is the rate I will pay both before and after any default described in Section 6(B) of this Note.

3. **PAYMENTS**
   (A) Time and Place of Payments   *[callout: due date]*
   I will pay principal and interest by making a payment every month.
   I will make my monthly payment on the **1st** day of each month beginning on **June 1, 2020.** I will make these payments every month until I have paid all of the principal and interest and any other charges described below that I may owe under this Note. Each monthly payment will be applied as of its scheduled due date and will be applied to interest before Principal. If, on **May 1, 2050,** I still owe amounts under this Note, I will pay those amounts in full on that date, which is called the "Maturity Date."
   I will make my monthly payments at

   or at a different place if required by the Note Holder.
   (B) Amount of Monthly Payments
   My monthly payments will be in the amount of U.S. $_______

   [callout: principal & interest (does not include escrow)]

4. **BORROWER'S RIGHT TO PREPAY**
   I have the right to make payments of Principal at any time before they are due. A payment of Principal only is known as a "Prepayment." When I make a Prepayment, I will tell the Note Holder in writing that I am doing so. I may not designate a payment as a Prepayment if I have not made all the monthly payments due under the Note.
   I may make a full Prepayment or partial Prepayments without paying a Prepayment charge. The Note Holder will use my Prepayments to reduce the amount of Principal that I owe under this Note. However, the Note Holder may apply my Prepayment to the accrued and unpaid interest on the Prepayment amount, before applying my Prepayment to reduce the Principal amount of the Note. If I make a partial Prepayment, there will be no changes in the due date or in the amount of my monthly payment unless the Note Holder agrees in writing to those changes.

5. **LOAN CHARGES**
   If a law, which applies to this loan and which sets maximum loan charges, is finally interpreted so that the interest or other loan charges collected or to be collected in connection with this loan exceed the permitted limits, then: (a) any such loan charge shall be reduced by the amount necessary to reduce the charge to the permitted limit; and (b) any sums already collected from me which exceeded permitted limits will be refunded to me. The Note Holder may choose to make this refund by reducing the Principal I owe under this Note or by making a direct payment to me. If a refund reduces Principal, the reduction will be treated as a partial Prepayment.

6. **BORROWER'S FAILURE TO PAY AS REQUIRED**   *[callout: grace period]*
   (A) Late Charge for Overdue Payments
   If the Note Holder has not received the full amount of any monthly payment by the end of **15** calendar days after the date it is due, I will pay a late charge to the Note Holder. The amount of the charge will be **5.000 %** of my overdue payment of principal and interest. I will pay this late charge promptly but only once on each late payment.

   (B) Default
   If I do not pay the full amount of each monthly payment on the date it is due, I will be in default.
   (C) Notice of Default
   If I am in default, the Note Holder may send me a written notice telling me that if I do not pay the overdue amount by a certain date, the Note Holder may require me to pay immediately the full amount of Principal which has not been paid and all the interest that I owe on that amount. That date must be at least 30 days after the date on which the notice is mailed to me or delivered by other means.

THE NOTE ALSO KNOWN as the Promissory Note, is a legal document that serves as evidence of a customer's promise to repay a mortgage loan. It outlines the terms and conditions of the loan, including the principal amount borrowed, the interest rate, the repayment schedule, and any penalty clause.

SAMPLE VERBIAGE

"This is your Note. It is your promise to pay the Lender. Here is your loan amount, your lender, your interest rate, your due date and your principal and interest. Once reviewed, please sign the last page. Do not date please".

Most Lenders require that the Note is not dated. Review your instructions carefully.

SIGNATURE/NAME AFFIDAVIT

DATE

LOAN #

BORROWER

THIS IS TO CERTIFY THAT MY LEGAL SIGNATURE IS AS WRITTEN AND TYPED BELOW
(This signature must exactly match signatures on the Note and Mortgage or Deed of Trust.)

(Print or Type Name)   Signature

N/A

(Print or Type Name)   Signature

N/A

(Print or Type Name)   Signature

N/A

(Print or Type Name)   Signature

(If applicable, complete the following.)

I AM ALSO KNOWN AS

(Print or Type Name)   Signature

N/A

(Print or Type Name)   Signature

N/A

(Print or Type Name)   Signature

N/A

(Print or Type Name)   Signature

and that   are one
and the same person

State of
County of

Subscribed and sworn (affirmed) before me
this   day of

Notary Public in and for
the State of
County of
My Commission Expires:

The Name Affidavit, also known as Signature/Name Affidavit, is a legal document used identify any and all other names the borrow is known by.

SAMPLE VERBIAGE

"This is your name affidavit. These are all the various ways your name appears on your credit report. Please sign the way it appears to the left".

For instance if the customer's name is

John Doe – he signs John Doe

John David Doe – he signs John David Doe

Notice of Right to Cancel

Lender	Borrower/Owner	Date

NOTE: All borrowers and owners must sign the Right to Cancel

Loan Number

Type

Property Address:

Date of transaction

Your Right to Cancel.

You are entering into a transaction that will result in a mortgage/lien/security interest on/in your home. You have a legal right under federal law to cancel this transaction, without cost, within three business days from whichever of the following events occurs last:

(1) The date of the transaction, which is ________ ; or

(2) The date you received your Truth in Lending disclosures; or

(3) The date you received this notice of your right to cancel.

If you cancel the transaction, the mortgage/lien/security interest is also cancelled. Within 20 calendar days after we receive your notice, we must take the steps necessary to reflect the fact that the mortgage/lien/security interest on/in your home has been cancelled, and we must return to you any money or property you have given to us or to anyone else in connection with this transaction.

You may keep any money or property we have given you until we have done the things mentioned above, but you must then offer to return the money or property. If it is impractical or unfair for you to return the property, you must offer its reasonable value. You may offer to return the property at your home or at the location of the property. Money must be returned to the address below. If we do not take possession of the money or property within 20 calendar days of your offer, you may keep it without further obligation.

How to Cancel. (Please include your loan number and printed name)

If you decide to cancel this transaction, you may do so by notifying us in writing, at:

End of rescission period

You may use any written statement that is signed and dated by you and states your intention to cancel, or you may use this notice by dating and signing below. Keep one copy of this notice because it contains important information about your rights.

If you cancel by mail, you must send the notice no later than midnight of ________ (or midnight of the third business day following the latest of the three events listed above.) If you send or deliver your written notice to cancel some other way, it must be delivered to the above address no later than that time.

I Wish to Cancel.

BORROWER IS NEVER TO SIGN HERE

_________________________ _________________________
Signature   Date

The undersigned each acknowledge receipt of two copies of this Notice of Right to Cancel and one copy of the Truth in Lending disclosures.

Each borrower/owner in this transaction has the right to cancel. The exercise of this right by one borrower/owner shall be effective to all borrowers/owners.

Borrower/Owner

Borrower signs and date

Date	Date

Date	Date

The Right to Cancel (RTC) also known as the right of rescission is a legal provision that allows customers to cancel certain types of loans with a three (3) day period after signing the loan documents. The right to cancel is designed to protect consumers from entering into loans they may later regret or fund unfavorable. RTC applies to loans secured by the customer's primary residence such as refinances and HELOCs. It does not apply to purchases or loans secured by investment properties.

SAMPLE VERBIAGE

"This is your Right to Cancel. By law you are given 3 business days in which you cancel the loan. Your 3 day will expire on ...... Please sign below acknowledging receipt".

IMPORTANT

DO NOT have customers sign in the section "I Wish to Cancel". If they do, replace those pages with their copies and have them sign them over in the correct place.

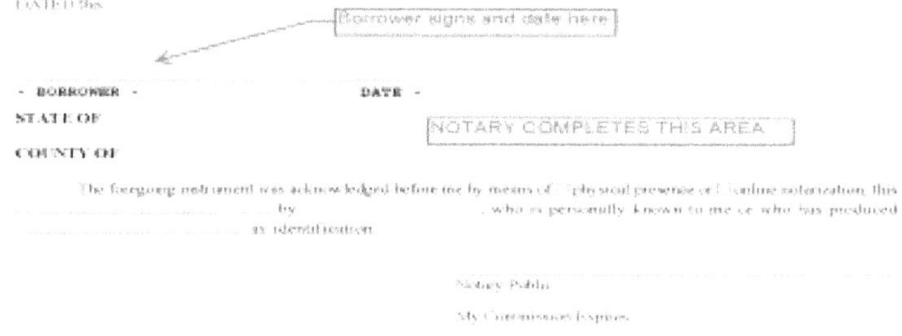

The Errors and Omissions Agreement is to establish the customer's co-operation to resign any documents as needed by Title Company or Lender.

SAMPLE VERBIAGE

"The Errors and Omissions Agreement is in the event there are documents which may need to be resign due to clerical errors or deem necessary, you will fully co-operate with the Lender or Title Company. Please sign and date".

CHAPTER 22 – ABOUT THE AUTHOR

L isa Carr

As a seasoned signing agent with over 15 years of experience in the field, my journey into the world of loan signings has been shaped by a rich background in the banking industry spanning two decades. My career began with a deep dive into the intricacies of banking, where I honed my skills in financial transactions, client relations, and regulatory compliance.

Throughout my tenure in the banking industry, I developed a keen understanding of the importance of precision and attention to detail in handling sensitive financial documents. My commitment to delivering exceptional service to clients and ensuring compliance with industry regulations served as the cornerstone of my professional ethos.

Driven by a passion for helping individuals achieve their homeownership dreams, I transitioned into the role of a signing agent in 2007, where I could leverage my expertise in banking to facilitate seamless and efficient loan signings. Over the years, I have had the privilege of guiding countless customers through the complexities of the loan signing process, providing clarity, support, and peace of mind every step of the way.

My extensive experience as a signing agent has equipped me with a comprehensive understanding of the nuances of loan documents, the importance of accuracy in documentation, and the significance of building trust and rapport with clients. Whether facilitating refinances, home equity loans, or purchase transactions, I approach each signing with professionalism, integrity, and a commitment to excellence.

Beyond my technical proficiency, I pride myself on my ability to navigate challenging situations with grace and diplomacy, ensuring that even the most complex signings are executed smoothly and efficiently. My dedication to continuous learning and staying abreast of industry developments has enabled me to adapt to evolving regulations and emerging technologies, further enhancing my effectiveness as a signing agent.

As I reflect on my journey as a signing agent, I am grateful for the opportunities I have had to make a meaningful impact in the lives of my clients and contribute to their journey toward homeownership. With over 15 years of experience as a signing agent and 20 years in the banking industry, I look forward to continuing to serve as a trusted partner and advocate for customers, lenders, and signing services alike.

I WANT TO EXTEND MY heartfelt gratitude to you for purchasing my eBook on becoming a successful loan signing agent. Your decision to invest in your professional development means a great deal to me, and I am truly honored to have the opportunity to share my knowledge and insights with you.

I believe that the journey to becoming a successful loan signing agent is both rewarding and challenging, and I am confident that the information and guidance provided in this eBook will empower you to navigate the complexities of the industry with confidence and skill.

Your support and commitment to your own growth are commendable, and I have no doubt that you will find value in the strategies, tips, and resources outlined in the eBook. Whether you are just starting out in the field or looking to enhance your existing skills, I am confident that you will find practical and actionable advice to help you achieve your goals.

Please know that I am here to support you every step of the way. If you have any questions, concerns, or feedback about the eBook or the loan signing industry, please do not hesitate to reach out to me. Your success is a priority, and I am committed to helping you succeed in your journey as a loan signing agent.

Once again, thank you for your support and for choosing to embark on this journey with me. I wish you all the best as you pursue your goals and aspirations in the loan signing industry. May this eBook serve as a valuable resource and guide on your path to success.

CHAPTER 23 - GLOSSARY OF TERMS AND ABBRIEVIATIONS

Jargons..........

1003 – Loan Application

4506 – IRS Tax Transcript Request Form

APR – Annual Percentage Rate

CD – Closing Disclosure

DTI – Debt to Income Ratio

E&O – Errors and Omissions Insurance

HELOC – Home Equity Line of Credit

HOA – Homeowners Association

LTV – Loan to Value

LSA – Loan Signing Agent

NNA – National Notary Association

NSA – Notary Signing Agent

POA – Power of Attorney

PUD Rider – Planned Unit Development Rider

QCD – Quit Claim Deed

RTC – Right to Cancel

RON – Remote Online Notary

TIL – Truth in Lending disclosure

Client – Lender, Title Company, Signing Agencies

Customer – Borrower, Seller, Signer

Loan Signing Agent

A professional who assists in the closing of real estate transactions by ensuring that loan documents are executed accurately and efficiently.

Closing

The final step in the home buying process where loan documents are signed, funds are disbursed, and ownership of the property is transferred to the buyer.

Loan Documents

Legal documents that outline the terms and conditions of a mortgage loan, including the promissory note, deed of trust or mortgage, and other disclosures.

Promissory Note

A legal document signed by the borrower promising to repay the loan according to the terms specified, including the principal amount borrowed, interest rate, and repayment schedule.

Deed of Trust or Mortgage

A legal document that gives the lender a security interest in the property as collateral for the loan. It provides the lender with the right to foreclose on the property in the event of default by the borrower.

Closing Disclosure

A document provided to the borrower before closing that outlines the final terms and costs associated with the mortgage loan, including loan amount, interest rate, closing costs, and other fees.

Right of Rescission

The legal right of a borrower to cancel certain types of loans within a specified period after signing the loan documents, typically three business days.

Errors and Omissions Insurance

Professional liability insurance that provides financial protection for signing agents against claims arising from errors, omissions, or negligence in the performance of their duties.

Notary Public

A public official authorized to witness and certify the signing of legal documents, administer oaths, and perform other notarial acts.

Identification Verification

The process of verifying the identity of signers by examining government-issued photo identification and confirming that it matches the information on the loan documents.

Closing Agent

The individual or company responsible for conducting the closing, including reviewing and explaining loan documents, collecting signatures, and disbursing funds.

Title Company

A company that conducts a title search on the property to ensure that the title is clear of any liens or encumbrances and issues title insurance to protect the lender and buyer against any defects in the title.

Escrow (Title Company)

A financial arrangement where a neutral third party holds funds or documents on behalf of the buyer and seller until all conditions of the transaction are met.

Escrow (Lender)

Lender collects a certain amount each month to pay taxes and insurance on behalf of customer.

Settlement Statement

A document that provides a detailed breakdown of the financial transactions involved in the closing, including the purchase price, closing costs, and adjustments for taxes and other expenses.

STAY IN TOUCH

Lisa Carr

service@lisasigningservice.com

www.lisasigningservice.com